Little Millie Affirmations On the Go

Dedicated to my Aunt Sheila,
my number one supporter and cheerleader. Auntie Sheila always believed in me, both as a child and as an adult, making me feel like I could do no wrong. Her love was truly unconditional. I know she's in heaven, smiling down on me always.

Little Millie's Affirmations On the Go remind us that we are worthy of love, joy, and growth, empowering our inner child to heal and embrace life's magic with confidence and hope.

I am enough,
just as I am today.

Little Millie teaches us
I am worthy of love and care.

I am strong, bold, and capable of creating magic in my life.

I am free to discover the joy and wonder of life.

I am learning to believe in myself, just like Little Millie does every day.

I am surrounded by love, and
I give it back to myself.

I am allowed to laugh, play, and feel excitement.

I am not perfect and forgive
myself for mistakes and
embrace a brighter future.

I am proud of myself and
who I am becoming.

I can rewrite my story
as many times as I need
to with courage and hope.

I am safe, and my inner
child feels safe with me.

I am growing and finding joy in every step.

I am strong enough to
turn my pain into growth.

I am choosing to shine, explore, and embrace all life's wonders.

I can turn challenges into stepping stones for a better tomorrow.

I am free to imagine and dream, like Little Millie always does.

I am healing my heart and discovering happiness along the way.

I am learning to trust myself
and my journey forward.

I am worthy of every good
thing coming my way.

I can heal my inner child with kindness and patience.

I am choosing to grow with love, light, and joy every day.

TAKE CARE OF YOU

THESE AFFIRMATIONS ARE SIMPLE YET IMPACTFUL, GREAT FOR BOTH KIDS AND ADULTS TO STAY MOTIVATED AND INSPIRED ON THE GO!

Scan QR code to enjoy the entire
Little Millie™ collection

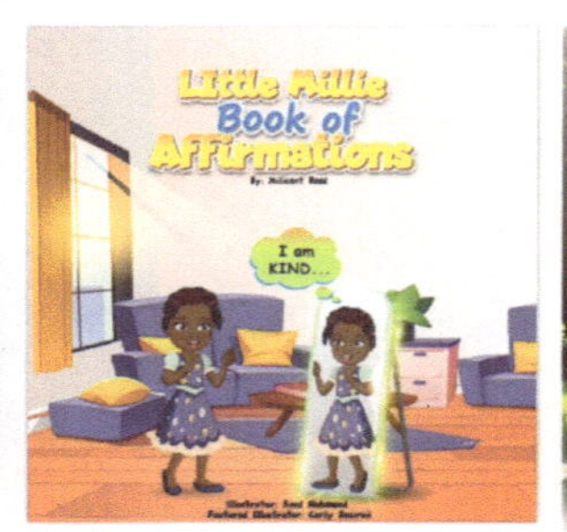

Written by Milicent Reed
Illustrator Meheryar

Published 2025

First printing edition 2024.
MDR Enterprise Holdings
PO Box 271743
Tampa, Florida 33688
www.mylittlemillie.com